The
World
Through
Tears

By Mary Beth Magee

Published by BOTR Press

Poplarville, MS

ISBN: 978-1-7378103-3-9

Copyright 2023   Mary Beth Magee
Published by BOTR Press
www.BOTRPress.com

Cover image formatted by Mary Beth Magee
Globe photo courtesy Library of Congress
Photo by Theodor Horydczak, ca. 1920-ca. 1950
Crying Eyes excerpt from Unsplash

The
World
Through
Tears

By Mary Beth Magee

Contents

From the Author

Sometimes the hardest part of pain is a sense of aloneness, the feeling no one else has ever hurt this way. The truth is, everyone hurts in one way or another. You do not weep alone.

You may have suffered the loss of a loved one, a possession, a job. Does illness plague you? Have you been injured, wronged, harmed by the actions of another? Does life disappoint you? You do not weep alone.

When we view life through our tears, we may lose sight of the larger world beyond our grief. Take a walk with me. We can get through it together. We do not weep alone.

Blessings,

Mary Beth Magee

Tears
for
Lost
Love

The Question

Missing you so much—

Why does one heart still beat on

Without the other?

Sorrow Poured Out

*Loss comes, not at a time we choose but rather when it will.
The cost of loving is the risk of losing the one you love. Lately, I
seem to be making payments too regularly. So, in tribute to
loved ones I've lost and those lost by ones I love...*

Too short, the time you spent here.
Too soon, our chapter closed.
Too sad, the weight of letting you go.
Too strong, the feelings I held for you.
Too beautiful, the joy of having you in my life.
Too hard, the task of going on without you here.

Telling you "Good-bye" and meaning it
Are two very different things,
Miles apart in accomplishment.
I laid a flower across your chest
And my lips said "good-bye,"
While my heart cried "Don't go!"

Although I know that God is in control
And loves you even more than e'er I can,
I wish He would have waited one more day
Before He called you from this world to His.
Yet I would have wanted even more,
Unsatisfied with less than "everything."

One day, the veil that separates our worlds
Will part and I will be there with you.
Our story will resume
And it will be as though no time had passed.
But the hours until then crawl slowly
And my "good-bye" echoes through my tears.

The Day You Left

The sun refused to shine the day you left.
Clouds filled the sky and drizzled on the place,
As if, like me, the universe bereft

Of joy, of life, refused to dare to face
A world where you would not be seen.
Life went from joyous gallop to a pace

Of foot-dragging crawl. Though I had never been
The one to beg or plead with fate, that day
I did. I tried to make a deal. Oh, what a scene

I caused, imploring God to make you stay.
But my request was not within His plan.
There's nothing left now but to simply say

Now you are gone. I'll never understand
How you could leave me, turn loose of my hand.

(a Terza Rima)

The Sweetheart Garden

We planted roses,
A promise of summer love
In red and green.

We planted peonies,
A dream of romance to live
For eternity.

We planted iris,
Blue symbols of hope and faith
In bright, bearded ranks

We planted daisies,
Innocence daring to reach
For heavenly joy.

I gather statice,
As I remember your eyes -
Sad, sympathetic.

I reap anemone,
As hope died when you did, and left me
Forlorn and alone.

Shell of a Heart

Once I had a beating heart --

Strong muscle, warm blood, hot emotions.

Once I felt a dream

Of warmth and caring and safety.

Long ago, I felt a love

Inflaming, carrying, lifting me.

Then there was the pain

Of crushed dreams and broken promises.

Like a seashell, empty and vacated,

My heart rests there --

A shell abandoned

Weeping for what might have been.

Whispers in the Night

I hear them calling,
The whispers in the night.
They echo horror's screams;
Reminders of the height
From which I've fallen,
Those pinnacles of love and joy
We two created in the dark.
Is there no spell I can employ
To regain those sweet, lost times
When you were mine?
Past dreams, once truths,
Have drawn a bloody line
Between what once was and what now is.
My sobs cannot block out
The taunting whispers chilling
My soul as they weave about
My heart. I've lost the fight
To keep you from the pit.
As once you embraced me
You now cling fast to It.
As Evil pulls you ever to its maw
I beg your heart, to no avail.
The whispers tell me you are gone
Forever taken beyond Evil's pale.

Slipping Away

You're slipping away
A bit more each day.
The harder I hold
The more I am told
"Let it go."

The person I love,
Fit like hand in glove,
Is pulling from me.
The distance I see
Seems to grow.

Precious moments fly.
I can only try
To treasure each one
Before you can run.
And I know

There will be a time
When our words won't rhyme.
Our paths will diverge,
My song become dirge
As you go.

Father's Day Memories

I had you for twenty-six years.
Years of joy and love,
Years of learning,
Years of growing.

You taught me about life,
And cooking and driving.
Late night card games
And John Wayne movies,
Louis L'Amour books and
Country music.

We sang together.
I square danced as you called the moves,
Left allemande and promenade home.
You taught me to bait my hook,
And to fish,
And to clean my catch,

You taught me so much.
Why didn't you teach me how much
Losing you would hurt,
Or how even though I've lived more than half my life
Without you,
I miss you still
And wish you were here
And want to tell you again,
"I love you, Daddy."

Lessons Learned the Hard Way

Once I thought you clever, witty,
Smarter than most.
But now I see through your wit
And can identify the cruel barb of hate.

Once I thought you handsome,
Most attractive of men.
But now I see the vanity of the image you cultivate
With your endless grooming tricks.

Once I thought you generous,
Lavish with your gifts.
But now I see how you sought to buy me,
To bind me to you with things and obligations.

Once I thought you noble, gracious,
Suffering from the mistreatment of others.
But now I know you earned their disdain
With tricks and cheats against them.

Once I thought you loved me
And wanted to share your life with me.
But now I know I was just another conquest,
A score for your cruel game.

Once I thought I loved you,
Putting you above all others.
But now I know I allowed myself to be deceived by
        you
And the cost has been my dignity, my sense of self.

Once I thought I couldn't live without you,
Wouldn't give up on the dream.
But now I know the nightmare has ended
And I can hold my head high as I walk away.

The Last Time We Loved

The last time we loved
I had no idea it would be the last time.
I didn't mark it on the calendar
    or note it in my diary.
Had I known,
I would have held on tighter, longer.
I would have inhaled
    more deeply of your scent.
Savoring each moment,
I would have memorized
    the line of your jaw,
        the velvet of your lips,
            the touch of your hand,
                the rough brush of your beard.
I would have whispered my feelings into your ear,
    told you how much you meant to me
        one more time.
But I had no idea.
You gave no hint.
I thought we had Forever.
The last time we loved
    marked the end of everything.
The last time we loved
    began a dark eternity without you.
The last time we loved,
    the last time I lived and breathed
        as a complete being,
            was the last time I existed
As something beyond a pale shadow.
Now I grieve
    for the last time we loved.
If only I had known...

Potentials

You might have been a rising star in corporate halls
        of fame.
You might have been an athlete, the true master of
        your game.
Perhaps an astronaut for you, with findings deep in
        space
Or part of filmdom's treasured few - a loved and well-
        known face.
A doctor or a soldier brave, fighting for others' needs.
You might have been a farmer, with your crops and
        stock and seeds.
My precious child, you once held such potentials
        without end.
But now there's only tears and pain which time will
        never mend.
The dreams, the hopes, the "maybes" died the day
        that I lost you.
You've taken with you all the visions I thought might
        come true.
I'll never see you reach those goals or others you
        might find.
The only place I find you now is deep inside my
        mind.
The best potential I could give you tore my heart
        right out,
But know that love decreed my choice, don't ever
        have a doubt.

I said goodbye and let you go to live another life.
You'll never know the tears I shed or feel the awful
      strife
Within my heart to give you up. Please know I love
      you so.
No matter where potentials lead, my prayers for you
      will go.

The Hole

A heart-shaped hole
at the center of my universe
Draws me in
As powerfully as a tidal bore,
As inexorably as a super-giant black hole.
I circle the edges,
Drawing nearer with each orbit,
Pulled ever closer.
The darkness there calls me.
The emptiness is not there,
But here, in my arms
Where you were meant to be.
In the darkness, will I find you?
In the darkness, will my emptiness be filled?
My precious child,
You left a void which can never be filled.
You left a longing which can never be quenched.
Losing you changed the landscape of my life forever.
I ache with the torture of your absence, but
Oh, I would not have missed loving you
For anything in the world.

Lives and Intersections

On the day we met, I gave it no great thought at first.
I'd met others who had no lasting impact.
But this time I was wrong.
At the intersection of your life with mine
The world changed, as though some celestial
chemistry occurred.
What if I had not been there that day?
What if you had gone another route?
Life would have been less textured, less beautiful.
At the intersection of your life and mine,
The sun was shining in a cerulean sky.
The flowers were blooming in a riot of color and
fragrance.
Our paths crossed there by chance –
Or was it?
Did heaven decree our meeting in advance?
At the intersection of your life with mine,
The world changed from "me" and "you" to "we."

But I should have remembered
An intersection has both an entrance and an exit.
Over time, we traveled from "we are" to "we were."
As we passed through
The intersection of your life and mine
To our individual roads, the world changed once
more
And I was alone again.
I wonder if I would have let myself
Intersect with you if I had known what lay on the
other side
Of the intersection of your life and mine.

Tears
for
Society

Let me in

Don't shut me out of your world.
Let me in, so I may experience it, too.
Don't tell me I don't get it and turn away.
I want to get it, I really do.

Don't feel as though you're the only one wronged.
Others have felt pain as well.
Don't let your pain fester and eat you.
Share your story with me, but don't yell.

History is filled with past injustices.
No group has been immune to wrong.
Please don't let history's errors
Take away your joy, your song.

I want to be on your side, an ally,
Not an enemy across some unseen battlefield.
We can face the world together, as one,
Have each other's back and shield

Against the misery born of division,
Against the despair born of hate.
Let me in and I will let you in.
We can find peace. It's not too late.

Each of us, a child of God,
Can claim royal lineage in our veins.
Through Him we can make peace at last
And counter loss with loving gains.

Honorable Mention, 2022 Mississippi Poetry Society Contest
Edition

Lessons Lost in Time

There were no banners waving when the deed was
      done;
No proud parades to honor those who fought.
Only faces wearing masks in dark of night
To bear a witness to the work they wrought.

Once labeled heroes, now their names are cursed.
Old actions, viewed as crimes and sins these days,
Were previously held in high regard.
But times have changed, and under modern ways

These men are judged by different rules and found
Wanting. The monuments once raised must fall.
Ignore the value of the artist's hand.
Bring down the statues which once stood so tall.

Rename the streets, forget the names once borne.
Relabel schools which once recalled their deeds.
We cannot learn by history ripped and buried.
Instead, the rewrite changes with the needs

Of those who now forget the men who sold them,
And blame instead the men who bought to build.
Though owners were not blameless, they bear all the
      stain
And good they did lies tarnished, prestige killed.

"Let he who is without sin," says the Bible.
Imperfect, yes, but they led, building by their hand.
Go visit them, in exile, if you dare be seen
Among the fallen heroes of the rewrit land.

Second Place, James George/Jefferson Davis Award,
Mississippi Poetry Society 2018

We All Hurt

I don't know what you've been through.
I wasn't there to see the slings and arrows you've
        endured.
You faced injustice, I know.
You suffered terrible wrongs.
My heart aches for your pain,
although I cannot feel it for you.
But I have been hurt, too.
My own road has tripped me and trapped me
and thrown roadblocks in my way.
I've lost some battles, won a few,
called others a draw.
We can stand, fists raised,
and try to prove who has been hurt more.
We can dredge up ancient wrongs to make a case.
As we list the past injuries,
we can each try to persuade the other
we were the more wronged one.
How can we compare wounds?
How can we measure each other's pain?
What does the comparison accomplish?
Better to open our fists
into helping hands.
Better to drop our arms
around each other's shoulders
and say, with truth and heart,
"I am so sorry for what you've known.
Take my hand.
Let's change the future together,
so no one knows such hurt again.
We are kin, children of God.
We are family."

Mary Beth Magee

Words

Lest we forget how often words can hurt,
Remember they can cut sharp as a knife.
Best take a moment now to think them through.
The careless lines bespoke can end a bond.

Let kindness be the measure of your words.
One moment's pause may stop a cruel retort.
Get gentle words to tell the things you feel.
Hone every sentence on the stone of love.

No later words can wipe out painful jibes.
Undoing harm may not be in the cards.
So, take a breath before you speak your thoughts.
Run then toward the peaceful and the kind.

Keep close the harsh words you would firstly say.
Deep pain avoid by speaking love instead.

(A "breaking the rules" sonnet with the rhyme at the start of the
lines rather than the end.)

Honorable Mention – Alabama State Poetry Society Award
(2022)

Masks

We all wear masks of some kind,
Whether we acknowledge them or not.
Some use physical masks as precaution,
Protection from smoke or germs or chemicals.
Masks to keep you safe from me or
Me safe from you,
Or both.

Other masks save lives more directly -
An oxygen mask gives needed breath,
An anesthesia mask provides blessed relief.
A mask of makeup hides so much -
Old scars or freckles or winter pale skin.
Who doesn't want to look their best
When facing a possibly hostile world?

Some masks lurk below the surface,
Perceived rather than seen.
Masks of emotion rather than substance,
They govern actions by coloring attitudes.
The mask of conceit and ego
Tries to conceal a sense of insufficiency
Behind a wall of false self-confidence.

The mask of bigotry fails to hide
Fear and ignorance behind its haughty dogmatic
facade.
Shyness hides behind a mask of indifference.
Meanness peeks out from behind the false front of
cruel humor.
Rudeness pretends to be "cool"
Or "witty" or "clever."

Mary Beth Magee

Look behind the mask of self-righteousness
And find anger, selfishness or hate.
Some use a mask of fake kindness
To hide a face of controlling behavior.

We all wear masks of some kind.
Some masks offer kindness and help.
Some offer harm.
We all wear masks.
Which mask do you wear?

Common Ground

If I reached out in friendship to you,
Could we meet on some common ground?
Or would old enmities keep us apart?
Would ancient hurts bring our best efforts down?

Generational scars we both bear.
Can we use them as common ground?
Let's rise above the wrongs of the past,
Lest ancient hurts bring our best efforts down.

Looking back at the lessons we've learned
We can meet on that common ground.
Yet brandishing them as clubs o'er our heads
Lets ancient hurts bring our best efforts down.

We cannot mankind's history undo.
Wrong was done, and by that we're bound.
If we go forward sworn to do right,
Then ancient hurts cannot bring us down.

So, I reach out in friendship to you,
Offer peace as our common ground.
May we, as brethren, walk forward as one,
And ancient hurts be buried and down.

Tears
of
Remembrance

Love and Death

Love doesn't end with death.
It just stretches a little farther
And reaches from here to Heaven.
Love doesn't die with the loved one.
The seed has been planted
And the flower of love waits
For the right moment
To burst into bloom again
In Heaven's garden.
Love renews itself,
Like a butterfly emerging from a cocoon.
Love doesn't stop with the last heartbeat.
The rhythm of the dance simply changes.
Love, once truly found,
Cannot be lost,
Only out of sight for a time.
Love provides the compass
To show the road back to each other
In God's time.

Originally shared on Facebook, 2018

At the Wall

Stately granite, angling from the earth,
Smoothed and polished,
Filled with dignity.
Mighty words etched into your surface.

You capture attention as you rise,
Demanding notice as you climb for heaven.
The green blanket at your feet offers beauty
But no warmth.

As you call us to remember.
You call us to heed the names.
You call us to honor the fallen, and
Remind us to treasure the survivors.

Your stark lines form a diagonal horizon between
worlds,
A delineation between innocence and experience.
You overwhelm with your weight yet
Uplift with your content.

Those of our parents, children, siblings, friends
Represented on your face are gone from our sight.
But never gone from our hearts, and
Ever memorialized on The Wall.

My Mother in the Mirror

Today I saw my mother in the mirror.
I recognized her dour scowl, lips tight and down
turned.
I knew too well the pinched eyebrows and sad eyes.
How could her face be there?
She's five years gone, resting in an urn by my bed.
I thought her long past the sadness
And troubles which kept her so glum.

Then I realized the face was mine,
The lips, the eyes, the brows all mine.
But I know joy. I know happiness.
Little of sadness lasts in my world.
My life is not opulent, but it is good.
Why do I have my mother's tragic face?

Can the answer lie in genetics and heredity?
Musculature and facial structure, rather than emotion?
Did my mother feel the joy I feel,
Know the love I know,
And she just was not able to let it show?
Did she feel my love, in spite of our bickering?
Did she feel my care, even when I fell short?
Did she remember the joy of our fun times together,
Even as her mind slipped away?

I pray it so.
I pray she felt the connection in my touch,
The gratitude in my actions,
The love in my heart.
When I see her in the mirror, I wonder.
And I whisper to her likeness,
"I miss you, Mama. I love you."

Wakamatsu Girl - 1871

What did you see, Okei-San?
As your eyes scanned the horizon, what did you spy?
When you closed your eyes and dreamed, what did
          you dream?
Did you remember home, an island nation across the
          sea?
Did you miss the world you left behind?
Did you long for absent family and friends?
Carrying your precious silkworm eggs and mulberry
          saplings,
You arrived in California to start a new life.
A new home awaited you on the American River,
A new colony of tea growers and silk producers.
War and fighting were left behind.
In the Foothills of the Sierra Nevada Mountains,
A dream of a peaceful life began for a teenaged girl
And the members of her group.

For Okei-San, the dream ended too soon.
Her brief life burned away by a fever at nineteen,
She sleeps there, in the soil of what was Wakamatsu
          Colony.
As the first Japanese immigrant and the first Japanese
          woman.
Buried in American soil, she rests in dignity.
She lived there only a few years, working as a nanny, a
          servant.
Yet she is remembered with honor,
This girl of Wakamatsu.

She embodied a dream of something better,
A search for a place of peace and hope.
She represents every dreamer who came, before or
        after.
Sleep gently, Wakamatsu girl.
We remember.

In Memoriam

I know you —
I see you there, gnarled hand raised in trembling
        salute to a wrinkled brow.
Eyes glistening for those I'll never know.
Yes, I know you — as you are now.

I don't know you —
As the young man building hopes and dreaming
        dreams.
Eyes looking toward the future you want.
But tomorrow isn't what it seems.

And I can't know you —
Not as you stood, tall and proud, snapping a salute,
Eyes shining with determination and courage,
Bright as the spit shine polish on your boots.

I'll never know —
The hell you went through over there, and here
Once you came home, or what you live with every
        day.
The memories, the pain, the losses, through the
        passing years.

But this I do know —
Every freedom I have today — to speak, worship,
        live,
Go where I please as I please - was bought
At the price of all you had to give.

So each time I see the you that I know
Let me think on what used to be.

And God help me always to be thankful
For the gift you have given for me.

Presented to Villa Park Veterans of Foreign Wars Post 2801,
Villa Park, IL

Shadows of Vietnam

He came home whole in body, not in mind.
The scars upon his psyche left him tied
To dreams of horrors. He could never find
A way to save the friends he lost. He tried

To turn off feelings, let no others in.
He built high walls to keep the world at bay.
He turned to drinking - whiskey, rye, and gin.
But rest eluded him. Sleep would not stay.

Vietnam's voice maintained its siren call,
Would not allow him to turn life's new page.
Alone and battered, he lashed out at all
And hid himself behind a mask of rage.

Trapped in the horrors he could not unsee,
From Vietnam he could not be set free.

Second Place, Vietnam Memories Award, 2023, Mississippi
Poetry Society Spring Contest Edition

Pietà

Agony. The pain of it all.
My beloved son, my firstborn
Now a corpse in my arms,
His flesh bleeding and torn.

How will I go on from here?
Why should I desire to live
When they have taken away the One
To whom I offered all I had to give?

Now His blood dries on feet
And hands pierced by nails,
A brow clawed by thorns.
Rational thought fails.

He was God's own Son.
And yet they crucified Him,
Taunted, tortured and derided
As none stood beside Him.

Through mother's tears I hear
His whispered promise clear.
"The third day I will rise again.
Weep not, my mother dear."

And so, I hold the broken shell
Which once contained my boy.
But in His words, I dry my tears
And count this moment joy.

An ekphrastic poem inspired by Michelanglo's sculpture.

Summer Song

Alas, our summer song has sailed away,
Sunlit sheets billowing against an azure sky.
A whisper in the rigging calls farewell.
We struggle, shorebound, sadly left to cry

For songs unsung and melodies unheard.
Untold tales of pirates, life and friends
Are silenced as the current sweeps him on.
In time, even the grandest story ends.

The captain seeks a new horizon now,
An island warm where pain does not abide.
He sails ahead, a table there to claim
For those who follow on a later tide.

The party will go on, in Jimmy's name
As summer's song still echoes "Glad you came."

In memoriam and celebration of the life of Jimmy Buffett

First published on Facebook, 2023

Tears
of
Regret

I Saw You Today

I saw you today.
You glided through the door, wrapped in sunlight,
Your head angled in conversation as you entered.
My heart jumped with joy at the thought of your
             embrace,
And the hope you hadn't come alone.
I saw you today
And I waved across the room, filled with expectation,
Delighted at the prospect of time to spend with you.
I wondered in that instant how long you could stay.
Rising from my seat, I wove through the crowd
             toward you, quickly as I could move.
I saw you today
As you stepped out of the sunlight, into the shaded
             room,
My heart cried out in disappointment.
You raised your head and glanced my way.
I saw it was not you at all, only someone of similar
             height and build.
I saw you today
Through the eyes of my heart, I conjured your image
             before me.
With the hopes of a mother, I tried to bring you close
             enough to hold.
By the wishes of my soul, I saw you there, shining
             with the sun glow.
But hopes and wishes couldn't make it so and my
             heart broke.
I saw you today,
But it was not you.

Plans – For Ed

My best laid plans, so carefully made,
Fall down in harsh reality's face.
Intentions cannot overcome
The anchor-drag of commonplace.

The daily jobs demand my thoughts
And fill my time with minor tasks.
The calendar and clock run on,
No care for boons my poor heart asks.

Then death, which overrules all time,
Steps in and takes a loved one's hand.
In shambles lie those well-intentioned
Thoughts of acts I might have planned.

"I should have" and "I wish I had"
Accuse me of my fallen schemes.
To say "I love you" one more time
Would be an answer to my dreams.

I laid my plans but failed to act.
The things I meant to do, undone
Until too late. Now grief wells up,
And sadness blocks the brightest sun.

Farewell, dear one. Forgive me, please.
I loved you and I always will.
Until the day we meet again,
Within my heart I hold you, still.

First appeared in The Tunica Voice newspaper, 2023

Remorse

I've made a royal mess of things this time.
How can I ever right the wrongs I've done?
I flounder now, like some demented mime.
Here in the dark, I find no trace of sun.

The people who believed in me, I've failed.
When they find out, they'll cast me from their hearts.
I think, by rights, they'll want to have me jailed
Or use me as a target for their darts.

I've lost it all – the world I worked to build,
The trust of those who counted on my skills.
The love of my sweet children I have spilled
Like ground-up husks from wheat in flour mills.

If only I could feel some good might come…
Then to despair my soul would not succumb.

Inspired by the character of George Bailey – "It's a Wonderful Life" (1946)

Song of the Wind

The shrieking wind whips past my door
To drape a cloak of bitter cold
Across the gray-locked landscape poor.
My arms wrap tight, scarce warmth to hold.

The lonely keening of the draft
Around the building corner serves
To leave my heart aggrieved, bereft.
It strums across my tightened nerves.

I hear the sorrow carried there,
And feel the tears the dark clouds weep.
The wailing sadness, hard to bear,
Comes from a broken spirit deep,

As if all hearts that ever broke
And shattered dreams of centuries long
Were gathered up and used to stoke
The piercing wind's mad howling song.

The shrieking wind drags me along.
It fills my heart with grief and pain
Until I seek death's final song.
I do not wish to feel again.

Secrets

Do not tell me your secrets.

Keep your guilty moments to yourself.

Push your skeletons back into their coffins

And do not rattle the bones at me.

I will not carry the burden of your past,

The weight of your sins.

I will not accept responsibility for protecting your
dark corners.

Do not tell me your secrets.

My shoulders already bow under the weight of my
own.

First Place, Free Verse Award, 2021 Mississippi Poetry Society
Fall Minifest

Haunted -- by More Than Ghosts

My heart is haunted --
Not by ghosts or goblins,
Or any such ephemeral creatures.
No, my heart is haunted by regrets.
Regrets for what I didn't do,
     but should have.
Regrets for what I wouldn't do,
     but could have.
Regrets for things I did that gave pain or sorrow.
Regrets for what I didn't see that needed seeing,
For calls I didn't hear that needed hearing,
Words I didn't speak that needed saying,
For emotions I shut down that needed feeling.
I grieve for paths I should have followed but didn't
     trace.
Regrets for people I've left behind
     or missed the chance to know,
Because I let other things become more important for
     the moment.
Regrets for time I wasted,
     sunsets I didn't see,
          flowers I didn't smell.
So many experiences un-lived and now regretted.
A priest could exorcise a demon or a ghost.
Garlic could stave off a vampire.
But nothing can change the past,
And so I must face the fact.
Regret
     will always inhabit my world,
Haunting my heart.

First appeared in the Tunica Voice newspaper, 2023

Irish Eyes

He was a right scoundrel, he was,
With a twinkle in his eye.
An incorrigible flirt, he teased me with a slightly
            naughty,
But not really offensive smile.
His graying hair did nothing to lessen his charm.
A few extra pounds looked well on him.
"Is your husband Irish?" he asked, a question
            prompted by my surname.
"I have no husband anymore. The name is my own."
"That explains your Irish eyes," he quipped,
And launched into the appropriate song.
From that day on, he serenaded me each time we met
            in our writing group.
He would end his rendering with a wink and a smile.
He called me Irish Eyes
And coaxed me to smile – if I wasn't already grinning.
Our innocent flirtation continued for months,
Two senior citizens with more need of friendship
            than romance.
One day, I noticed his clothes hanging
A little looser than usual on his frame.
When I asked his weight loss secret,
He sighed. "Complications of diabetes.
But I'm working on it. Don't you worry."
He began missing meetings.
Word came to us that he had lost a leg to the
            complications.
I went to visit him in the rehab center,
Hoping to cheer him.
When I entered, he gave a weak but welcoming smile.
"I've missed singing to you. May I sing to you now?"

"I've missed hearing you," I answered.
And he sang our song again, his voice a weak echo of
        the past.
"You do, you know," he said when he was finished.
"Your Irish eyes always make my day brighter and
        better.
Thank you for sharing them."
"Your song always does the same for me," I said.
I kissed his cheek before I left.
I didn't see him again. Two days later he died.
Now my Irish eyes smile–but sadly–missing my
        roguish friend.
Irish tears flow freely whenever I hear the song.
But I remember him singing it, and I smile again.

Grief and Joy

Today I went to say goodbye to a friend.
My heart ached, and those around me echoed
The pain, the grief, the sadness.
His life had been filled with
Goodness, kindness, generosity.
All who knew whom were blessed
By the experience.
When illness came to sap his health
And slow his steps,
He only slowed, he didn't stop.
I grieved the pain he suffered,
The difficulties he endured,
The failed procedures meant to help.
I grieved the hurt his family felt,
The helplessness to fix things,
The desire to spare him.
Now I grieve his absence,
The hole left in the world by his passing,
The loss his family and friends feel.
But I feel only joy for him.
Joy for his healing in heaven,
Joy for his restoration to all he had been
And more!
Happy home-going, my friend.
Joyous eternity, dear fellow.
I'll see you soon at the Father's table.

Tired

Another call,
Another message of loss.
Someone I care about has lost a loved one
Or crossed the bridge from life themselves.
It hurts, God, it hurts like crazy.
The older I get,
The more the world spins out of control
And I lose them, one by one, heart by heart.
I'm so tired of saying goodbye,
Of letting go of a relationship I treasure.
So tired of investing in another,
Only to have my emotions dashed.
So tired of hurting and watching others hurt.

But the price of not hurting is too high.
To keep my heart safe would cost
The joy of knowing and loving another.
The only way to not lose is to not love
And not loving is a loss in itself.
I am tired of losing loved ones,
But I pray I never tire of loving the ones
God sends into my life.

Tears
of
Hope

The Battle

In the darkness of the night, questions assail me.
How can I keep going, when all I kept going for is
        gone?
What can I do when what I have done for so long no
        longer needs doing?
Where do I place my efforts, when the one I worked
        so long to help has left me behind?
My tears pour out in a river of defeat and grief, my
        best efforts shattered ruins of failure.
In the quiet of my heart's darkness comes the answer.
I will never leave you or forsake you. You are not
        alone.
The one you love is safe within my arms,
Gone from your sight but not your heart or my
        care.
You will be together again.
Carry on, there is other work for you to do in my
        kingdom.
The light of my love will guide you on, if you will
        only follow.
Be comforted.
This victory is won.
Claim it and rejoice.

Originally appeared in the "Inspire Victory" anthology, 2014

Finding Her Power

Emerging
    struggling,
    fighting from the womb
    of life's woes, she comes.
Battered by contractions of misfortune
    she rides the riptide of
    unfaithful lovers
    and demanding employers.
In a world unkind
    to women of a certain age, she dares
    to look beyond the bloody limits
    set by others,
    to gaze upon the bright sun
    of possibilities.
Head clear of the birth sac,
    she draws a deep breath
    of the air of freedom and identity.
She pushes, strains and births
Her new self.

An ekphrastic poem inspired by *Cadmium Sea* by Barbara Dani

Between the Doors

How do you feel when a door closes?
Do you hear an angry slam or gentle click?
Does the sound of the door feel condemning
Or encouraging, like a friendly hug?
There are doors between worlds and lives
And opportunities and stages.
Until the door closes on one,
We may not be free to move to the next.
No door closes on <u>everything</u>.
Each doorway provides exit to one thing
And entrance to another.
Do not grieve the closing of a door.
Celebrate, instead.
Rejoice for the next stage of being.
When the door closes behind you,
Stride boldly forward into the future.

Heaven Will Be Pink

Heaven will be pink, I'm sure,
For those we lost before the cure
Was found. 'Til then, we walk and pray,
Keep them in our hearts each day.

Keep the research going strong.
We'll do our part to move along
The process as the cure is sought.
Stand fast with those who battles fought

With drugs and rays and scalpels bright.
When the final answer comes to light
We'll celebrate God's healing love
For those still here or gone above.

Begin Anew

I have made mistakes.
I've tripped over my own intentions.
I've fallen on my face.
Sometimes, I've caused others to fall
Because of my actions
Or inactions.
Much as I regret these failings,
I can't undo them.
But I know one saving secret, one precious truth.
I can begin anew in Christ's love.
I can start again, fresh and clean,
Forgiven my past weaknesses and missteps.
I may fall again.
I'm human and fallible, after all.
But my new beginnings offer hope
I can do better in the future.
So I begin anew,
Christ's newborn child.

Honorable Mention, All Things New Award, 2023 Mississippi
Poetry Society Spring Contest

The Calf

She dragged the carcass of the dead calf,
Bloated, blackened tongue out, fly covered.
Out of the pasture, away from the tiny herd,
She pulled the body.
A cloud of insects followed the smell of death.
The old cow plodded behind,
Lowing as her daughter was taken away.
Into the woods, the woman proceeded.
The old draft horse protested its morbid load,
Snorting and stomping as the woman insisted.
When they reached the little hollow,
She backed the horse a step to slacken the rope.
Once she released the calf's hind legs,
She leveraged the body over the edge and into the
hollow.
As her hope for a profitable season slid down the
decline, she wept.
For the dead calf, the childless cow, her own dreams,
she wept.

A flock of butterflies descended on the carcass,
Seeming to promise hope in the midst of calamity.
She straightened her spine, dried her tears on her
shirttail,
And turned back to the business of farming.

About Mary Beth Magee

Mary Beth has been writing poetry as long as she can remember. She is a member of the Mississippi Poetry Society as well as several other writing groups. Her works have appeared in many anthologies and on several websites as well as in volumes of her own work.

The World Through Tears marks an effort to reach out to those who grieve for any reason and let them know they are not alone. If her words have comforted you, encouraged you, uplifted you she has achieved her goal.

Poetry Books by Mary Beth Magee

Songs of Childhood, Echoes of Years

Life and All – The Journey

For more about her other books, visit her website at www.LOL4.net.

www.ingramcontent.com/pod-product-compliance
Lightning Source LLC
Chambersburg PA
CBHW071347290326
41933CB00041B/3042